How Jewish Laws and Customs Develop Over Time

A Fascinating Explanation by
Rabbi Edward M. Gershfield

Edited, with an Introduction, by
James N. Gershfield

ABOUT SCRIBAL SCION PUBLISHING

Scribal Scion Publishing LLC was founded in 2022 by James N. Gershfield as a tribute to his late father, Rabbi Edward M. Gershfield, of blessed memory, who passed away in 2019.

Rabbi Gershfield was an eminent Jewish legal scholar, professor, lecturer, Gittin expert and scribe, and gifted orator and preacher.

The company mission is to publish works of Jewish non-fiction for a diverse audience with the aim of increasing understanding of Jewish religion, law, customs and culture.

To learn more about the company, or to submit a request to join our email list, please visit:

https://scribalscionpublishing.com

Other books by James N. Gershfield:

The Illuminated Omer Counting Book

How Jewish

Laws
and
Customs

Develop

Over Time

A Fascinating Explanation by
Rabbi Edward M. Gershfield

Edited, with an Introduction, by
James N. Gershfield

First Edition published in 2023

Paperback ISBN-13: 979-8-88665-002-0
Hardcover ISBN-13: 979-8-88665-003-7

Published by Scribal Scion Publishing

Scribal Scion Publishing is an imprint of
Scribal Scion Publishing LLC

https://scribalscionpublishing.com

Contents

Dedication

This book is lovingly dedicated to the memory of my late father, Rabbi Edward M. Gershfield, who passed away in December, 2019, after a long life imbued with the love of learning and teaching Torah, that is Jewish Law. Originally from Winnipeg, Manitoba, Canada, Rabbi Gershfield moved to New York City at a young age to pursue his Rabbinical education and ordination at the Jewish Theological Seminary of America, and he stayed at the Seminary as a Professor of Talmud and Rabbinics for the rest of his career.

In the Mishnah, Bava Metzia, Chapter 2, Mishnah 11, it says: "Your father is the one who brings you into this world, but your Rabbi is the one who teaches you wisdom and helps you to get into the world to come". In my case, both were true: my father was my Rabbi, and my Rabbi was my father.

"B'Ezras Hashem Yisborach", which is Hebrew for "With the help of The Blessed Name", as my father used to say, may this be the first of many books that I will publish containing his teachings, so others can benefit from his deep understanding and easy-to-understand explanations of the Torah, which ultimately is a guide for the proper way to lead one's life.

Introduction

This book contains a lightly edited version of a lecture given by Rabbi Edward M. Gershfield in the early 1970's to students in a post-graduate course on Jewish Jurisprudence. But please don't get scared by the word Jurisprudence! It comes from two Latin words: juris, meaning "of the law", and prudentia, meaning "prudence or good judgement". The word jurisprudence can be defined in various ways, but a simple definition is "a philosophy of law". Studying jurisprudence means studying the terms, principles and methods that help us to understand various legal systems. Thus, Jewish Jurisprudence encompasses the terms, principles, and methods of the Jewish system of law.

Rabbi Gershfield was a pioneer in the

use of technology, especially tape recording, for educational purposes. Because of his foresight in taping this lecture, we are now able to enjoy reading his words of explanation of these very important topics.

At the time that Rabbi Gershfield gave this lecture, he was already a very fine Jewish legal scholar, having graduated from the Rabbinical School of the Jewish Theological Seminary in 1958, and having received a DPhil (Doctor of Philosophy) degree in Comparative Roman and Jewish Law from Oxford University in England in 1965, in addition to Masters degrees from Columbia University in Latin and in Education. When he spoke about Jewish Law, he had the ability to bring to bear his wide knowledge of non-Jewish legal systems in addition to his extensive Jewish legal knowledge and understanding.

Introduction

One of Rabbi Gershfield's greatest strengths, and probably the thing he enjoyed doing most in his career, was teaching. He was able to explain complex ideas in simple terms and in a lively and approachable manner. He used to say, partly jokingly, that taking a simple idea and making it complicated is "scholarship" whereas taking a complicated idea and describing it in simple terms is "genius". His ability to connect with students is clearly demonstrated in this lecture, which was intended for advanced students of Jewish Law but can still be understood by those who do not have formal legal training.

The specific topics discussed in this lecture could be discussed at great length, but Rabbi Gershfield distills the essence of these topics and provides examples that help us to understand the concepts involved.

Introduction

Two main topics were discussed in this lecture: Authorities of Jewish Law and Custom in Jewish Law. Each of these topics is contained in a separate chapter in this book.

The first topic addresses the question of how legal decisions are made in Jewish Law, what "legal authorities" are, and how these compare to legal decision making in other legal systems. The second topic explains what "customs" are within the context of Jewish Law and how customs can take on the force of law in certain circumstances.

At the time that this lecture was given, Rabbi Gershfield was a member of the Committee on Jewish Law and Standards (CJLS) of the Rabbinical Assembly affiliate of the Jewish Theological Seminary of America, and the lecture includes an interesting explanation of how that committee discussed questions that were submitted to it, and how it arrived at its legal decisions.

The astute reader will notice that some words in the text are underlined. This indicates a vocal emphasis that Rabbi Gershfield used when speaking, as can be heard in the original tape recording. In addition, in a few places the English grammar appears to be incorrect; however, that is because Rabbi Gershfield spoke to the class in a semi-impromptu way and was not reading from a written script. In preparing this lecture for publication, I wanted to preserve the feeling that one would get when sitting in the classroom listening to the original live lecture.

Before jumping into the lecture, I want to provide some background, so that you will be able to understand better the terms and ideas mentioned. I have also created a Glossary at the end of this book with definitions of many of the Hebrew and legal terms used in the lecture.

Jewish Law has a number of "layers" to it. First, there is the written Torah, also known as the Five Books of Moses, which is the basis or foundation for Jewish Law. Second there is the oral Torah, preserved in the Talmud, and which consists of two main parts: the Mishnah, which is a collection of statements of laws, and the Gemara, which contains the legal discussions about the laws that are stated in the Mishnah. There are also comments on the meaning of the terms and statements of the Gemara. These are known as the Tosafos, which is the collection of elucidations on the Talmud written by Jewish scholars in France and Germany in the 12th and 13th centuries. Those scholars are known today as the Tosafists.

Introduction

The term D'Oraisa is mentioned in the lecture. This is an Aramaic word that means "from the Torah". If a law is "from the Torah" it means that the law is part of the combined written and oral law that was received by Moses on Mount Sinai. Laws that were added later by the Rabbis are called D'Rabanan, which means "Of the Rabbis", and carry only slightly less weight than laws that are D'Oraisa.

A number of major codifications of Jewish Law were created later, one of the most well-known being the Shulchan Aruch which was written in the 16th century by Rabbi Joseph Karo in the Land of Israel.

In addition to the codifications of Jewish Law, over the past several centuries many Rabbis have written Responsa to questions that were sent to them about specific cases and how to rule in those cases according to Jewish Law. Responsa are called Sh'eilot U'teshuvot in modern Hebrew, and Shailas and Tshivos in Yiddish. Rabbi Gershfield grew up in Winnipeg, Manitoba in Canada, speaking Yiddish at home and learning Talmud in Yiddish in the Talmud Torah school as a young lad. So, when he used to talk about Responsa as an adult, he would say the Hebrew words using a Yiddish pronunciation.

The word for Law in Hebrew is "Halachah", which comes from the Hebrew word meaning "walking along a path". That is, the Jewish Law tells Jews what the correct path is to take in their lives. Customs, on the other hand, are called "Minhagim" in Hebrew, and a single custom is a "Minhag". The word "Minhag" comes from the Hebrew three-letter root N-H-G, which means "to drive", and it refers to the way in which Jews have "driven" down the path that has been set by the Jewish Law.

Another thing that is mentioned in the lecture is the observance of the Jewish holidays. The general Hebrew term for any Jewish holiday is "Yom Tov", which literally means "a good day". In the Land of Israel most of the Jewish holiday days are only observed for a single day, while outside the Land of Israel it has been customary for many centuries to observe two days of Yom Tov for each Jewish holiday day. The one exception is the Jewish New Year, known as Rosh Hashanah in Hebrew, meaning literally the "head of the year", which is observed for two days both inside and outside the Land of Israel.

Finally, I added words in square brackets here and there to help make the meaning clearer.

And now, please take your seat in the classroom, as the lecture is about to begin.

Authorities of Jewish Law

This field is a very wide, and enormous, subject, because every national group and every legal system has a very complex way of creating its law. And they are not the same for everybody. They are not the same from period to period. They change historically. So, the whole problem is extremely complex.

But the main areas of investigation are clear, and among them are: Legislation, Custom, Precedent, Equity and so on. There is another one that I would like to add, and that is "Interpretation of Laws".

The English, or the Anglo-American, system of courts, that is the judicial arrangement, is based primarily on precedent. That is to say, the binding law upon one court, aside from the written statutes that are created by the legislator, whoever that legislator might be, but the great <u>body</u> of law that is applied is really decided cases of previous courts. And this is called a "common law".

And in the common law, all sorts of principles are developed over the course of time, through judicial decisions. And these decisions become precedent for further decisions. Every once in a while, legislation either consolidates all of this decision, or upsets it, or reverses it, or whatever it is, depending on the constitutional relationship of the legislative power and the judicial power in any particular state.

However, in the civil law systems, that is to say those systems built on the basis of Roman Law, namely Europe, Central Europe, principally

France, Germany, and Italy; and those countries, that is, modern states that have adopted civil law systems, such as the Communist governments of Russia and China, which by the way adopted a civil code; and Japan, which has adopted a civil code, modeled very closely on the French and German codes; and of course, the offshoots of Central European civilization, such as all of South America, which is built on Spanish and Brazil and Portuguese legal systems, which are the same type as the Central European.

Now, in this system [of civil law], which is by far the greater one in numbers in the world, they don't have the great reliance on precedent. That is, a court is not bound by the precedent of a previous court. The court is bound by the <u>law</u>.

The law is stated in a code. And the <u>code</u> is binding. And the code may consist of a very short piece of literature, such as the German civil code, which is one of the shortest in existence. And that is one of its great usefulnesses, that it is so concise, and it's very abstract and short, and it can be applied with a tremendous <u>variety</u> of applications.

So, the court is bound by the <u>code</u>. And then the code is <u>interpreted</u> by experts, or "jurists" as we might call them. Now these jurists are not judges. Mostly, they are law professors, or they are just people who happen to be learned in the law. And they can express an opinion on how they understand the code. And it may be that a certain court will decide that the code means "such and such and such" in this particular case.

It may be that later on a jurist, a professor, or just a writer on the subject, will express an opinion that the court was <u>wrong</u>, and it should be interpreted differently. And if this is generally found to be acceptable among experts, then the next time such a case comes up it may happen that the court will say that the previous court made a wrong judgement on this, and the law really should be something <u>else</u>, and <u>this</u> is the proper way it should be.

So, the way you argue before a court in a civil law system is you cite, not authorities of previous courts, but authorities of <u>experts,</u> that is you quote what is called "authorities". Professor So-And-So in his book on This interprets the code in such-and-such a way. And the <u>study</u> of the code, in the law schools, reflects this.

In common law systems, in the United States and the British Commonwealth, generally - with the exception of such places as the Province of Quebec, which has a civil code, and the State of

Louisiana, which has a civil code, and also New Mexico, I believe, which has certain <u>parts</u> of the law in a civil code - aside from these throughout the English speaking world, you have that the law training consists of learning the system of precedents. That is to say, learning the leading cases on each particular subject. Where are those important cases from which the principles were drawn to rely upon in future cases, and so on. So, what you do is you learn all the leading cases, let's say all the cases on torts, all the cases in contracts, the cases in wills, the cases in so-and-so, how the court interpreted, and that is how you build up your knowledge.

In French law schools, or German, or Spanish, or Venezuelan, or Japanese law schools, what you learn is the code <u>and</u> the authorities that have interpreted it. What you learn is the Gemara [which contains the legal discussions in the

Talmud] and the Tosafos [that is the collection of elucidations on the Talmud which were written by Jewish scholars in France and Germany in the 12th and 13th centuries] rather than the Shailas and Tshivos [that is the "Questions and Answers", or Responsa written by Jewish scholars in response to questions about specific cases]. It's quite a different way of operating.

Custom in Jewish Law

Now, custom affects these systems quite differently, as you can obviously imagine right away. The code, those areas where the code is the basic law, they don't really want to take so much cognizance of custom. Because they want to put the "center of gravity" in the <u>code</u>. Whereas the common law puts, I think, considerably more weight on custom. Where there isn't judicial precedents or legislation to abolish custom, and so on, then custom is also a kind of precedent that we rely on, and so on.

Now, what I want to do is bring this around to the Jewish Law. In Jewish Law, you can see on the basis of this discussion that we rely very heavily on a kind of civil law system – a system of code and interpretation. First of all, historically we don't have any legislatures, right now - we used to, but we don't now. And if Jewish Law is to be made <u>now</u>, it can <u>only</u> be made through interpretation of existing codes, or using previous decisions as material, as "authorities", for the interpretation of the codes.

Now, this is how we operate with the Shulchan Aruch, very parallel. When the Law Committee gets a question, on some obscure point, what we do is we say "What is the <u>law</u> on this? Does the <u>Torah</u> say anything about it?" No, it doesn't. "Does the <u>Talmud</u> mention it?" Well, something <u>like</u> it, maybe, obliquely. "Well, do our codes, does Maimonides, the Shulchan Aruch, do <u>they</u> mention it?" Maybe they do, maybe they don't. Suppose they do, and suppose there are contradictory codifications on it, suppose we have different opinions. What we do then is we <u>balance</u> the authorities, and we try to understand the interpretations, what is the best interpretation for <u>us now</u>, to apply to <u>this</u> case.

And on occasion, we have said that, whereas the law has been understood to be such-and-such, let's say the law of the <u>Sabbath</u> has been understood to mean such-and-such with respect to certain <u>work</u>, previously, nowadays we have new inventions and gadgets and mechanical devices which were not contemplated by our ancestors, and therefore what we try to do is apply the kind of <u>general</u> approach that they would have, to try and see what the law should be in <u>this</u> case.

Now, I don't think we're <u>new</u> in that. We didn't discover it, the only thing that <u>we</u> do is we tend to be very <u>conscious</u> and deliberate about it. Whereas, in previous ages, this tended to be more "under the surface", and the <u>formality</u> of making everything appear as though it existed in the code, was much stronger before. We don't feel so <u>compelled</u> now to say that Moses in his wisdom saw every problem of the internal combustion engine, and the flow of electricity from a hydro-electric plant to my toaster, and so on. So that we don't feel compelled to <u>prove</u> that.

But, in effect, what we are doing is that we say that Moses received the Torah which, when properly interpreted, will provide us guidance in settling such problems. So that when we decide to turn on the ignition switch on some machine or not, because it's Shabbos, what we're doing is <u>obeying</u> the Law of Moses. We're not obeying the law of the Law Committee, but that this is part of the continuing formation of Jewish Law.

This is constantly going on. Authorities have differed throughout the ages. And what happens is that eventually there is a sort of consensus within the communities to which ones we will follow and which ones we won't. Some things we can leave in a controversy and some things we can't.

So, in the course of time what happens is that, in a kind of "custom" certain decisions become adopted, and others don't. This is what I was driving at. When you come down to the specific question, "What is the place of custom now in Jewish law, in Jewish history?" Well, there is an <u>enormous</u> significance in custom, because it is so important – we don't have formal legislation, we don't have formal precedents, because no Rabbi or Rabbinical Court is really specifically <u>bound</u> to follow some other Rabbinical Court or decision. There is no power that binds them to it. You can't be impeached because you don't render proper decisions. And what we end up with is a kind of reliance on custom.

Now, "minhag" has been noticed many, many times by many writers as being a very powerful element in Jewish Law. And everyone who writes books about Jewish Law mentions minhag. So, all the standard books on it will talk about it. [Asher] Gulak and [Isaac] Herzog and so on, and [George] Horowitz. But no one has really penetrated the effect of custom in relation to <u>other</u> legal systems. And I think that is a very valuable thing too.

For example, recently we had a big discussion in the Rabbinical Assembly about the second day of Yontif. Now, second day of Yontif is stated pretty clearly in the Talmud to be a <u>custom</u>. And we have a very interesting debate, which I am sure everyone is familiar with, in [Tractate] Beitzah – so what do you do when the calendar was in trouble, we didn't know when the date was, so we set up a bonfire and so on, and then the Samaritans set up "counter" bonfires, and they mixed us all up with the beacons. And, anyway, we added another day, just to be sure, and so on.

Now that we know how to fix the calendar, we don't need all of the beacons. This whole telecommunications system is superfluous. So, the Gemara ends up with the conclusion "Well, we still have it because Maaseh Avoseihem Beyedeihem" [the actions of their ancestors are in their hands]. The people have more or less adopted this custom because that's the way it's been done for some time now. And the effect is time immemorial because we don't know <u>when</u> this custom started.

By the way, "time immemorial" in English Law has a specific date, when time immemorial begins. It begins in the year 1189, in the time of King Richard. You remember him, the Lion Hearted, The Great Crusader. In his time, some judges early on ruled that if a custom could be proved back to the time of King Richard, that's enough. So that eventually that became accepted as time immemorial. If you want to prove something, you have to prove that it went back to the time of King Richard. Normally, you don't have to prove that every person from that time did it, but you have to prove that there was no time from 1189 when the custom was <u>not</u> observed, or was abrogated, or abandoned, and so on.

So, in a sense, the Yom Tov Sheni is a typical kind of a creation of a legal custom, from time immemorial. And there was an attempt to either put it on a legislative basis, or to try and read it back into the code, or to abolish it, and so on. And the result was, in the Talmud, anyhow, that it <u>stuck</u> because people – it became customary to observe a second day of Yom Tov.

Now, what we do about it now? If we would have a sort of comparative approach, I think we would have a much clearer way of thinking about how customs work and operate. We would not be compelled to go into a lot of debate about what is a custom, when do you abrogate a custom, and so on, and looking for out-of-the-way statements and Tosafos and some other such places, when we could adopt a much simpler theory of custom, by noticing that all peoples have this problem of customs, and it's perfectly legitimate to have customs, and there are more or less reasonable ways of dealing with it, and it would save us a lot of debate.

Let me point out a couple of things. In the Talmud, in the Mishnah, there are various places in which custom is the basis of a definite claim, a monetary claim. For example, in Bava Metzia, in the Mishnah, we have a number of cases where people hire workmen. And they hire them on certain conditions. You hire, let's say, in the certain season, when the ground is hard to work, in the rainy season, so if you hire them in the dry season you can't make them work in the rainy season, and so on. There are certain things that you do.

Or let's say a worker is entitled to be given a meal on the day that he is working. Why? Because of "Minhag HaMedinah". And the Medinah doesn't mean "the kingdom", it just means "the countryside", that community. So, if a person can prove, look if the custom in this area is that when I rent a piece of land that, or let's say when I rent out a piece of land to you for one season, and we will share the crop, it is a custom that after the crop is out, that you will plow up the land, and you return it to me with a final plowing. That's to make sure that there are no weeds left, and seeds, and so on, and it breaks up the weeds. Now, if you <u>don't</u> do it, I can <u>force</u> you to do it, or else I can have it plowed and send you the bill. Because that is a <u>Minhag</u>. And the Minhag meets some of these criteria – it's an <u>old</u> Minhag, an <u>accepted</u> Minhag, it's reasonable and lawful, and all that sort of thing.

Now, when you study the code, I think that what follows is that you should be able to distinguish what things have come into the code through interpretation of previous texts, and what has come in through custom.

Recently somebody asked me about this problem: What is the origin of the rule that we don't cook fish and meat together? Now, for fish and meat, there is no rule in the Torah anywhere that forbids mixing fish and meat. But we don't cook it together, and it's a custom not to eat it together. You can have it at the same meal, but not together. Separate courses, but you don't mix them together. Now, if you look in the books, you will find that it goes back to a statement in the Gemara that eating fish and meat is dangerous to your health. It's a "Sakana" [a dangerous thing].

Now, it became a custom not to cook fish and meat together. And the codes clearly state that. On account of Sakana, it is customary not to. Now, recently a doctor comes up to me and says, "I've been reading in the Shulchan Aruch", one of the rare birds that reads the Shulchan Aruch, and he says "and as far as I can tell there is no medical evidence whatsoever that eating a piece of fish at the same time as a piece of meat is going to do you any harm, at all".

This custom is obviously, clearly, based on some kind of medical understanding. Now, if we can say without any hesitation that our medical knowledge is much clearer than it used to be, although there are still a lot of things that we don't know, but on this point the best physicians of our time are convinced that it won't make you sick. Not only that, but it won't do you any harm at all. So, what remains for this custom? Now, as long as people continue to observe the custom, so nothing happens. Its reasonableness is now demonstrated not to exist. It was a "mistaken" custom. There is nothing <u>wrong</u> with it.

But now, suppose somebody would want to say or raise a question at the Law Committee: "I would like to prepare a dish that consists of this kind of mixture. May I, or may I not?" And this <u>has</u> come up. So, what do we say? We say to them, and this is how we have answered them in the past, that the books say it is a Sakana, and we tend to doubt it, and if you really want to do it, probably nothing will happen to you. But it is <u>customary</u>, it has become a custom, not to do it. If you want to abide by the custom, etcetera. So, you can see how custom finds its way into the law, but it can just as easily find its way <u>out</u> of the law once the underlying assumptions change.

Sometimes you get a <u>bad</u> Minhag. And we have many bad Minhagim. For example, let's say in England, suppose the Parliament in England decides that a certain custom is harmful. Let's say the custom of burying the wife <u>alive</u> with her deceased husband is not a nice custom. And we ought to stop it. So, what they do is they pass a legislation making this illegal. Let's say they find people betting on cock fights. Well, that's an old custom, so they find that this is illegal. Or bear baiting was on old custom. So, that became illegal. So, you can <u>abolish</u> customs by legislation.

Our problem is we don't <u>have</u> legislation. We don't have the <u>machinery</u> for legislation. How do you abolish customs like that? Well, what you do is you stand and you make a Kol Korei [meaning, a public statement], you take an advertisement in the Morgn Zhournal, and <u>yell</u>. For example, many Rabbis protested the custom of reciting Kol Nidrei. At the very beginning, Kol Nidrei was a source of terrible <u>embarrassment</u> to Judaism. You stand up and you say "Kol Nidrei VeEsarei VeCharamei", all of these statements, vows, oaths, promises that I will make MiYom Kippurim Zeh Ad Yom Kippurim [meaning, "from this Yom Kippur until next Yom Kippur"], "Y'Hei Betaeilin U'mvutolin", [meaning, "they should be null and void"], nothing, and nobody can rely on my promise. And if I promise things, or take vows or oaths, forget about it, I don't mean it.

Well, we can put a historical face on it and say that we are talking about Marranos and forced conversions. But some people, who would like to seize on an occasion like this, will say "No Jew can ever be trusted in anything he says, because every Yom Kippur he has a secret meeting and gets together with his congregation, and they have a conference there, where they say all this stuff I am going to say, etcetera". But that custom <u>stuck</u>, and it stuck because there was religious motivation for it. There <u>were</u> such religious persecutions, and people <u>did</u> have to make sort of outward concessions to foreign practices in order to stay alive or keep their businesses and so on.

So, what we did is we, that is we the

Rabbis, we just had to go along with it. And we put the best face on it that we could. We say that Kol Nidrei is a very <u>nice</u> prayer, and solemn. And in any sermon, I would venture to guess, out of all the people here who speak on Yom Kippur, very few of us ever mention the literal meaning of the words that this is going to make our promises worthless, and so on, and emphasize <u>that point</u>. We avoid that; we try to put a religious content into it. And that's how we <u>save</u> such a custom.

Or take the custom of Kapores [that is, waving a chicken over one's head in preparation for Yom Kippur]. And by the way, funeral customs are <u>many</u>, and some of them really are <u>bizarre</u> and <u>crazy</u>. Some of them are actually practices of Avodah Zarah, real idolatrous practices. So, whenever we can we try to abolish them. If we had a means of legislation to abolish it we could, but we can't. Or this business of praying to the sprits of the dead.

Take, for example, in the Tosefta of Shabbos, there is a whole chapter on Darkei HaEmori. Now, Darkei HaEmori means "customs of the Amorites". These are the symbols of the pre-Israelite occupants of Palestine. Now, there's a whole bunch of customs there, you see a whole list of them that are forbidden on the grounds of Darkei HaEmori. About Chapter 7 or 8 or so in the Tosefta of Shabbos. Not the Mishnah.

Now, there you have Darkei HaEmori. For example, when you start plowing your field in the Springtime, the first thing you do is you get some other guy to come and start plowing and he says some certain mumbo-jumbo and try to fool ..., well you don't do this. Or to grow hair in a certain fashion which was an imitation of the priests of some of the cults that they had. And all kinds of these superstitions.

Now, these customs, these are customs, but they were forbidden, as much as the Rabbis <u>could</u> forbid them. But anyhow, the force of custom in Jewish law is <u>tremendous</u>. And it's one of those <u>juggernauts</u>. It moves in certain ways. And you can sort of push it a little this way and push it a little that way, but you can't really <u>start</u> it and you can't <u>stop</u> it.

What about the custom of Bat Mitzvah? Now, that's not from time immemorial. That is from "time Kaplanian" that he invented [referring to Rabbi Mordechai Kaplan, the founder of the Reconstructionist movement in Judaism]. Now, how long is it going to be before people will say that there is a Jewish custom of Bat Mitzvah? In certain circles, we do already, in other communities they don't.

Or, the late Friday night service. It's a custom, I think. Isn't it? But, there are many communities where the late Friday night service is being <u>abandoned</u>. It became customary in certain places, and then for some reason it became <u>not</u> customary. Or, some Rabbis now are adopting the custom of "doffing" robes while they are conducting services, so that they should look like everyone else in the Shul. Now, there are reasons why Rabbis put on robes, and there are reasons why Rabbis want to keep away from robes. But all these are <u>customs,</u> and you just can't stop them.

When we try to cite authorities, from Shailas and Tshivos, it is <u>precedent</u> in a sense, but it is precedent in <u>interpretation</u> of the code. It's not that because Rabbi Nodeh B'Yehudah [the name of the work of Rabbi Yechezkel Landau of the 18th century] rules so-and-so, therefore all the Hungarian courts have to rule that way. It isn't so. They only follow his opinion because he was considered a great expert, and very knowledgeable, very wise, and if he interpreted the law to be <u>such,</u> then that shows that so-and-so. His decisions are very authoritative. Or other very fine old Rabbis. Now, if we find that their interpretations are not appropriate to <u>us,</u> then we can have the temerity to say "Well, that was very good for the old days, but nowadays we look at it differently."

There is no doubt that it is precedent. But the precedent is used as a convincing interpretation of the law. You see, it is very different from saying that the courts of the State of New York are bound to interpret the 14th amendment in a certain way <u>because</u> the Supreme Court of the United States has interpreted it that way, and its interpretations are binding upon the State courts. It's not because when the State court has a problem it considers that Chief Justice Earl Warren was a great Talmid Chochem [meaning, a Great Sage], and we ought to abide by <u>his</u> decisions because he was very <u>wise</u>. As a matter of fact, it doesn't matter, it's completely irrelevant if he was wise or wasn't wise. The binding nature of precedent is built into the American <u>system</u>.

But we don't do that. We don't say that we have a hierarchy of decisions and courts, and we have a system of binding decisions and precedents. What we do is we can say, as some Rabbis do, that in the last 500 years the only intelligent decisions that were ever made were by the people [the commentators] who were printed in the little Oysios [meaning, "letters"] alongside the Shulchan Aruch. And that since that day [of the printing of the Shulchan Aruch] the only thing we can do is study the old authorities. Of course, it's just a cover up, because after all they <u>do</u> have to decide <u>now</u>, and we do have scholars now, but they take the <u>pose</u> of being completely helpless and having to go back to the old authorities, and so on. And the greater the authority the better.

Now, that's not <u>precedent</u> in the Anglo-American sense, in the common law sense. That's precedent in the sense of <u>interpretation</u>. This is found in the Mishnah itself: "The law is such and such and such and such and such. Maaseh B'Rabban Gamaliel [meaning, "a case that came before Rabbi Gamaliel"], who did so and so and so." And if Rabban Gamaliel did it, then everybody knows that really <u>is</u> the law.

The expression "Minhag K'Din Hu" [meaning, "a custom is like a law"] is just a short-hand expression of saying that there are times when a custom has the force of law, because if you tried to deter people, they won't pay any attention to you. It has no force whatsoever. It's the sort of thing that an American Rabbinical authority made a statement that a Jew is forbidden to pray on Rosh Hashanah in a Synagogue where men and women sit together, in spite of the fact that that's the only possibility you would have to hear the sound of the Shofar, which is D'Oraisa. Well, so what happened when this authority spoke up? So, a lot of people who wouldn't ordinarily go to Conservative congregations were confirmed in their belief not to go to a Conservative congregation. As far as I can see, no great effect was had upon the attendance at Conservative congregations. Those people who go there anyhow continue to go there, and those who wouldn't have gone in the first place didn't go. And I think that out of the 5 or 6 million American Jews I think there was one fellow who actually wrote a letter to that authority asking him his opinion. <u>He</u> was the <u>only</u> person involved who <u>acted</u> on the basis of this opinion, as far as I can tell.

Now, the reason why I mention that is that people are in the habit of acting the way they're acting, and it's <u>very</u> difficult to deter them. It's difficult to get them to <u>come</u> to Shul, and it's difficult to get them to <u>stop</u> coming to Shul. If a Rabbi would undertake a program to abolish every second Shabbos, let's say just bi-monthly Sabbaths, he just couldn't do it. There is no power on earth that would prevent people from doing it. Or if he says "We want to abolish the custom of saying Kaddish [a special prayer that mourners say in the Synagogue] except for during the month of December. Then we'll say Kaddish, one month a year". Well, he can say all he wants, he can stand on his head. All such proposals to <u>change</u> customary behavior have to take this into account. It's an enormous problem.

It's not a statement of <u>law</u>, it's a statement of <u>analysis</u>. It's a statement of an historical <u>judgement</u> upon the law, but it's not a law itself. I'll give you an example of the sort of thing I have in mind. In the 19th century there grew up a practice in Germany and then elsewhere, to turn some of the prayers in the Synagogue into the language of the country. To pray in German. Or to give a sermon in German. And, of course, in other languages. Now, this struck many Rabbis at the time as very <u>bad</u>, a very bad practice.

So, what they did was they turned to the ancient sources. Well, to their astonishment, they took a look in Masechet Soitah [a tractate that deals with the laws of a woman who is suspected by her husband of committing adultery] in the

Mishnah, and they saw a whole list of things that you can say in any language you want. Kriat Shma [meaning, "reading the prayer that begins with Hear O Israel"] in Kol Loshon [meaning, "any language"]. You can say the Shma prayer in <u>any</u> language you want – you can say it in Chinese, Bulgarian, <u>but</u> Birkas Hamozon [the Grace After Meals prayer] you need to say in [Hebrew]. Now, there are rules, and there are ancient precedents for it. That's chapter 7 of Soitah.

Then it says that Parshat Sotah has to be said <u>Bilshonah</u> [meaning, "in its language"]. There is the question, "What are the things that need to be said Bilshonah and She'einah Bilshonah [meaning, "not in its language"]?" And there is a whole discussion in the Gemara whether you can read the Torah in other languages, and so on. Now, the modern problem of praying in foreign languages. It became customary over many generations to pray in Hebrew in a certain form. And when you appeal to the old text, you won't find ammunition for stopping them. And by the way, Shema specifically is B'Chol Loshon SheAto Shomeya [meaning, "in every language that you hear"]. The Gemara is very clear on that.

There is one opinion, Rabbi Yehudah Ha-Nassi, and the Chachomim. The Chachomim say "any language". And that's the Halachah, in every code. So, you can go into any Reform Synagogue in the world, and I'm pretty sure you will hear all kinds of languages, but the Shema, that you'll hear in Hebrew. Everything else you'll hear in other languages, but the Shema you'll hear in Hebrew. That's the one part, and there is no doubt whatsoever, that you can say it in any language.

We get an argument now in Israel why

you can't have a Kesubah in Hebrew. Or why we can't have a Get written in Hebrew. I have no doubt whatsoever, that the words Shema Yisroel can be put into any language on earth. The fact of the matter is, that it is <u>permitted</u> to do it, according to the <u>law</u>. Now, whether the custom puts a certain kind of value upon saying it in its original language, for whatever reason it has, it became customary to say it in Hebrew <u>only</u>, and so on. But these customs, now. Oh, so why do I mention it? Rabbis in the 19th century <u>defended</u> the custom of praying in Hebrew on the basis of it being now a long-accepted custom. And they said, even though you can prove from all kinds of texts, that you can say anything you want in any language, it is a very great <u>Mitzvah</u> to keep our custom. And that is all it amounted to. That really is the basis of their whole argument. And many of our practices are defended that way.

It's not a technical question of time immemorial. They have appealed to custom, and they said "well, by <u>now</u> it's a custom to do this this way and we mustn't change". And that is a very <u>strong</u> argument. And it's a <u>good</u> argument. Because, generally speaking, customs <u>are</u> reasonable. And the fact that a certain thing became a custom is probably based on a very rational and understandable purpose. That people <u>did</u> have a <u>need</u> to do it that way. Now, whether they <u>still</u> have that need, or the needs are still satisfied by doing in <u>that</u> particular way, instead of some other particular way, that is questionable. And you have to examine each custom as it comes.

Customs which are <u>public</u>, they have to be regulated. For example, a group of Yemenites, and others, came to Eretz Yisroel [the Land of Israel], with large families. Half of the family consisted of children and the other half wives. And this is not according to <u>our</u> custom. We Ashkenazic people, we have, at least since the time of Rabbeinu Gershom, if not earlier, have <u>abandoned</u> this custom of having many wives. Now, what happened when people from different communities came together in Israel? Can you say to the Yemenites, "Get rid of all of your wives, pick one and get rid of all of the others", because <u>our</u> custom is, and so on?. They can say, that's very nice that you observe your custom but I and my father and my great-grandfather all the way back to the time of who knows who, we've been doing it this way. From time immemorial. And it's a very <u>fine</u> custom. All kinds of justifications can be made. It's got reasonableness, and everything. In fact, they don't understand how someone can get along with just one wife.

So, what did they do? They had to

legislate. The State of Israel, the Parliament, that is the Knesset, legislated this problem out of existence. What they did was, all those immigrants who come from Eidot that <u>have</u> this custom were permitted to remain married to their wives. But, people belonging to that community would henceforth not be permitted to contract polygamous marriages in Israel from that point on. So, it was a kind of attrition.

Now, this system of attrition was used in many disputes. What do you do when a labor contract calls for an engineer and a fireman on a locomotive, and then somebody invents a locomotive that can be operated by an engineer alone, and you don't need a fireman? So, what do you do? Do you fire 50,000 firemen? The Canadian railways were one of the first to do this. What they did was a system of attrition. All the firemen now working would remain on the job, and no new firemen are hired. And as they retire or they leave the company, then they are not replaced, and in the course of time the problem is eliminated without hurting those people now involved. The same thing was done with the Yemenite immigrants.

Now, that you can do when you have a system of legislation, as in Israel. If that system doesn't exist, as in the Diaspora, then what we do is we just have to have a sort of amorphous system of customs, conflicting customs, and it's a constantly changing, constantly difficult thing to manage.

Reasonableness is subjective, because reasonableness must also mean reasonableness now, not just reasonableness when it started. But it has to remain reasonable. For example, it may be a custom that people should honk their horn when pulling away from the curb. You can imagine such a custom. Now, maybe when cars were first started and you wanted to scare a horse that was blocking your path, you would toot at them. But nowadays this has caused a great deal of racket, and unnecessary noise. So, <u>now</u> it is <u>not</u> reasonable any more to have such a custom. In those places where it is still reasonable, you do it. If there is a difference of opinion, then it is controversial.

Glossary

Ashkenazic: Originating from, or related to, the geographical areas of France and Germany.

Avodah Zarah: The words literally mean "strange service" or "strange worship". Idolatry.

Beitzah: Literally, an "egg" in Hebrew, refers to a tractate in the Talmud that discusses the laws of Yom Tov. The tractate is called Beitzah because that is the first word in the text of the tractate.

CE: Refers to the years of the Common Era (the current method of numbering the years).

Chachomim: Sages (plural of the Hebrew word "Chochom", meaning Sage). In the Mishnah, the word Chachomim is used to refer anonymously to the consensus opinion of the Rabbis.

D'Oraisa: An Aramaic word meaning "From the Torah". That is, a law which is either written explicitly in, or derived from, the Five Books of Moses, or is part of the Oral Law.

Diaspora: Anywhere in the world that is outside the Land of Israel.

Eidot: The Hebrew word meaning Communities (the plural of Eidah, a community).

Get: The word used in the Talmud to refer to a Jewish bill of divorce. The plural is Gittin.

Gemara: The discussions about the precise meaning of statements in the Mishnah, and their applicability to specific situations.

Glossary

Kaddish: The prayer that mourners recite at certain points in the daily services in the Synagogue. The Kaddish prayer can only be said in the presence of a Minyan.

Kesubah: Also pronounced "Ketubah". A Hebrew word that refers to the Jewish marriage contract. In modern times, the Kesubah is purely a religious document.

Law Committee: This refers to the Committee on Jewish Law and Standards of the Rabbinical Assembly.

Maimonides: Also known as "Rambam", which is a Hebrew mnemonic standing for "Rabbi Moshe Ben Maimon" (Ben means "son of"). Maimonides means "the son of Maimon". Rabbi Moses the son of Maimon was one of the most important Rabbinical authorities, and wrote major works on Jewish Law. He lived most of his adult life in Egypt and wrote works in both Hebrew and Arabic, but mostly in Arabic. Maimonides lived from 1138 to 1204 CE.

Minhag: The Hebrew word that means "custom". The plural, in Hebrew, is Minhagim.

Minyan: The quorum of 10 worshippers required in order for mourners to be able to say the Kaddish prayer during Synagogue services.

Mishnah: The Jewish oral law, which was written down around the year 200 CE. The Hebrew word Mishnah derives from the word that means "twice", or repetition. That is, the oral law was studied by repeating it over and over verbally so that it would not be forgotten. The word Mishnah can also refer to a single paragraph in the larger body of law known as the Mishnah.

Glossary

Mishnayot: The plural of the Hebrew word Mishnah.

Rabbeinu: A Hebrew word meaning "Our Rabbi", a term of great respect.

Rabbinical Assembly: The American association of Conservative Rabbis.

Rosh Hashanah: The Jewish New Year holiday, which is celebrated for two days.

Sabbath: The Jewish day of rest (Saturday) on which no work is permitted. In Hebrew, it is called Shabbat or Shabbos.

Sakana: Hebrew word meaning "a dangerous thing".

Shma: Hebrew word meaning "Hear!". It refers to the prayer that begins with the words "Shma Yisroel", Hear O Israel!

Glossary

Shabbos: One of the ways of pronouncing the Hebrew word that means Sabbath, the other way being Shabbat.

Shofar: A ram's horn, which is blown daily (except on Saturdays) during the month preceding the Jewish New Year, and on the days of the Rosh Hashanah holiday.

Shul: The Yiddish word meaning Synagogue.

Talmud: The combination of the Mishnayot and their related Gemara. In the Talmud, each Mishnah is followed by a section of Gemara.

Tosefta: A compilation of Jewish oral law that is separate from the Mishnah, but compiled around the same time period as the Mishnah. The Gemara often quotes from the Tosefta when analyzing statements in the Mishnah.

Torah: The Jewish Law. The Torah consists of a written law and an oral law.

Yiddish: A language that was spoken by many Jews in Europe in the 19th and 20th centuries.

Yom Kippur: The Jewish "Day of Atonement", which occurs nine days after the first day of Rosh Hashanah.

Yom Tov: A Jewish holiday (literally "a good day").

Yom Tov Sheni: The second day of a Jewish holiday. The word Sheni means "second".

Yontif: The Yiddish pronunciation of the Hebrew words "Yom Tov", shortened into one word.

Index

Index

Index

Index